T0065360

Also by Lucie Brock-Broido

Trouble in Mind, 2004

The Master Letters, 1995

A HUNGER

A HUNGER

POEMS BY

Lucie Brock-Broido

ALFRED A. KNOPF   NEW YORK
2014

THIS IS A BORZOI BOOK
PUBLISHED BY ALFRED A. KNOPF

www.randomhouse.com/knopf/poetry

Some poems in this work were originally published in the follow-
ing publications: THE ANTIOCH REVIEW, GRAHAM HOUSE REVIEW,
IRONWOOD, THE MISSISSIPPI REVIEW, NER/BLQ: NEW ENGLAND RE-
VIEW AND BREAD LOAF QUARTERLY, NEW LETTERS, SHANKPAINTER,
THE SOUTHERN POETRY REVIEW, and THE VIRGINIA QUARTERLY
REVIEW.

"Autobiography" and "A Little Piece of Everlasting Life" were
originally published in THE AGNI REVIEW.

"After the Grand Perhaps," "Domestic Mysticism," "Magnum
Mysterium," and "Ten Years Apprenticeship in Fantasy" were
originally published in PLOUGHSHARES.

Grateful acknowledgment is made to The Sheep Meadow Press
for permission to reprint the poem "In a Landlocked Time" by
Lucie Brock-Broido from A CELEBRATION FOR STANLEY KUNITZ by
The Sheep Meadow Press. Copyright © 1986 by The Sheep
Meadow Press. Reprinted by permission of The Sheep Meadow
Press.

Library of Congress Cataloging-in-Publication Data
Brock-Broido, Lucie.
    A hunger.

    I. Title.
PS3552.R6145H86   1988   811'.54   87–46036
ISBN 0–394–56337–9
ISBN 0–394–75852–8 (pbk.)

FOR MY FATHER
JOEL GREENWALD
WITH LOVE

Contents

(ONE)

Notes on some of the poems follow the text on page 58

Domestic Mysticism

In thrice 10,000 seasons, I will come back to this world
In a white cotton dress. Kingdom of After My Own Heart.
Kingdom of Fragile. Kingdom of Dwarves. When I come home,
Teacups will quiver in their Dresden saucers, pentatonic chimes
Will move in wind. A covey of alley cats will swarm on the side
Porch & perch there, portents with quickened heartbeats
You will feel against your ankles as you pass through.

After the first millennium, we were supposed to die out.
You had your face pressed up against the coarse dyed velvet
Of the curtain, always looking out for your own transmigration:
What colors you would wear, what cut of jewel,
What kind of pageantry, if your legs would be tied
Down, if there would be wandering tribes of minstrels
Following with woodwinds in your wake.

This work of mine, the kind of work which takes no arms to do,
Is least noble of all. It's peopled by Wizards, the Forlorn,
The Awkward, the Blinkers, the Spoon-Fingered, Agnostic Lispers,
Stutterers of Prayer, the Flatulent, the Closet Weepers,
The Charlatans. I am one of those. In January, the month the owls
Nest in, I am a witness & a small thing altogether. The Kingdom
Of Ingratitude. Kingdom of Lies. Kingdom of *How Dare I.*

I go on dropping words like little pink fish eggs, unawares, slightly
Illiterate, often on the mark. Waiting for the clear whoosh
Of fluid to descend & cover them. A train like a silver
Russian love pill for the sick at heart passes by
My bedroom window in the night at the speed of mirage.
In the next millennium, I will be middle aged. I do not do well
In the marrow of things. Kingdom of Trick. Kingdom of Drug.

In a lung-shaped suburb of Virginia, my sister will be childless
Inside the ice storm, forcing the narcissus. We will send
Each other valentines. The radio blowing out
Vaughan Williams on the highway's purple moor.
At nine o'clock, we will put away our sewing to speak
Of lofty things while, in the pantry, little plants will nudge
Their frail tips toward the light we made last century.

Domestic Mysticism

When I come home, the dwarves will be long
In their shadows & promiscuous. The alley cats will sneak
Inside, curl about the legs of furniture, close the skins
Inside their eyelids, sleep. Orchids will be intercrossed & sturdy.
The sun will go down as I sit, thin armed, small breasted
In my cotton dress, poked with eyelet stitches, a little lace,
In the queer light left when a room snuffs out.

I draw a bath, enter the water as a god enters water:
Fertile, knowing, kind, surrounded by glass objects
Which could break easily if mishandled or ill-touched.
Everyone knows an unworshipped woman will betray you.
There is always that promise, I like that. Kingdom of Kinesis.
Kingdom of Benevolent. I will betray as a god betrays,
With tenderheartedness. I've got this mystic streak in me.

Birdie Africa

for Stanley Kunitz

WOLF

My father calls me Wolf.
He says that I will see things other people will not see
at night. When he holds me, heat comes out
of his big arms & I belong to him.
In the cold of Christmastime he rocks
me in his deep lap in the great shadow of a comforter.
We are wool on wool,
back & forth, singing these songs
whose words I can't even say out loud.
I think they're about God who keeps us in his paws.
My mother watches, standing at my window, arms
folded to her chest. One fingerbone
of moonlight reaches in, tapping on the lock
of her face, restless, not like a mother wolf
but lit like she is going
somewhere else.
But when I wind my arms around
him, put my face into the dimmed scoop
of his neck, he smells like good warm fire
like dark sweet dreams.

THE ROOF

I sleep on the roof now.
She has taken me away from him.
I sleep thinking of his face tucked
next to mine like a big black bear.
There are other children now.
We run like wild
animals. We let our hair go
into puzzles which will never be unraveled.
We let our teeth go fierce.
We leave dirt in our palms
& sleep without nightclothes.
We pee in the yards & eat raw things.
In the dark we watch the traffic lights blinking
from our sleep in the cold night air.
Sometimes I talk to the stars

Birdie Africa

& the stars keep the traffic
in the sky from bottling up.
Each person gives off a little
torch when they sleep
& mine's the softest one.

BIRDIE

I am Birdie now I don't know why.
I squat at the edge of the top
of our rowhouse & I'm without wings I think.
Philadelphia isn't gentle now. Bad things echo up
& down our neighborhood at night.
I think we wound the people of our street.
I am hurting myself.
I can't tell time you know.

ALL THE AFRICAS

All the Africas live here
like a family of fire.
My mother always wears the bone of moon
across her face. I peer at her
like through a keyhole & I don't know why.
She never touches me.
The grownups eat cooked things
& we go foraging,
carving our designs in trees
& benches in the park & cedar picnic tables
left out in the trash, we never leave our names
& we can't read.
I am the clean seed
of a new race springing
from the dark continent of America.
God keeps me pure & savage here
before Moses
before the gift
before TV & toothbrushes
before the alphabet.

THE LAST AFRICA

The man with the megaphone warns Vincent Leaphart
to get out. He stays on, we stay here with him.
From up top of the bunker, the city
is our karroo dotted with colors of light.
In the dark, we are swept
down to the belly of our house.
They turn water on us
like a devil. We stay on.
We are flooding, there is no light left.
Then the fires & we huddle in the basement
under wet green blankets. Everything smells bad.
My mother stops twisting & I don't know why.
Everybody wailing. I am Birdie & I don't know how.
Then a quiet like I've never heard before.
Ramona Africa pulls me outside to the alley
& I burn there with her, naked on the stones
in the sweet jungle of the city.
When I come home my father will be singing
like an old kind dream. I have seen things
at night that other people have not seen.

Evolution

The extinct creatures would have liked this day,
a festival flooded all the way to the river.

If they were still alive with us, they would curl
into the leaves left from last autumn,
begin their long journey to be coal.
Someday, they would be precious minerals.

They might have been confused,
the cello playing solo,
these brief black strokes—
the Chinese character for rain.

But they would have understood
the love of old leaves heaped,
the dogs barking down
the late afternoons, howling for summertime.

What I want is to sleep away an epoch,
wake up as a girl with another kind of heart.

In the Vatican library, the letters
to Anne Boleyn are pinned down to keep
from coiling. An entire country
changed its faith once for its king.

I want to know what the letters say & go on
saying, what her face looked like in sleep.

By supper the invalids will be lying
down, whorled in white coverlets,
exhausted from yearning.
Everything they do is smaller than these
who walked in a world
that was greener than this one.

I am the medieval child in the basket, rocking.
Feigning sleep, up all night listening for secrets:
why there are punishments,
what news bad weather brings,
how things get winnowed out.

Real Life

Soon the electrical wires will grow heavy under the snow.
I am thinking of fire of the possibility of fire & then moving

Across America in a car with a powder blue dashboard,
Moving to country music & the heart

Is torn a little more because the song says the truth.
Because in the thirty-six things that can happen

To people, men & women, women & women,
Men & men, in all these things the soul is bound

To be broken somewhere along the line,
That clove-scented, air-colored wanderer blushing

With no memory, no inkling & then proceeds
Across America

In the sap green of the tropics,
Toward the cadmium of a bitter sunrise to a new age,

At the white impossible ice hour, starving,
Past the electric blue of the rivers melting down,

Above the nude, snuff, terra cotta, maybe fire,
Over the tiny fragile mound of finger bones

Of an Indian who died standing up,
Through the heliotrope of a song about the sunset,

To live the thirty-six things
& never comes home.

Ohio & Beyond

Towns pass like pretty girls you wish
you'd left behind, lifting their skirts gentle
against their legs—   *Ravenna, Elyria, Vandalia*
dark-haired beauties who fling their hair
like girls do when the weather up & shifts.

In Mingo Junction, spring will happen
easily. The first warm night hangs
on the eaves of the dancehall, drops
down to the wooden floorboards, settles
in the avocado vinyl of the front porch swing.

You met a girl here once
in the days when the land rolled back
& fields of coal bloomed forth & glistened.
Everyone was rich for a little while.

She played the jukebox for you here
one shiny night in April, curled her cool hand
around your fist, danced slow with you.
She said,   *I found a starfish once in Florida.*
Dresses stuck to girls' skins differently back then.
It wasn't all laid bare.

All the way from here to Newfoundland, the ripbop
on the car radio carries you, rises
like an ether, blue & faint on the road.

A Little Piece of Everlasting Life

I used to live in a train parked
In a yard in the middle of Virginia.
What I liked best about that era in my life
Was that the moon used to hunt us down
Come sliding in through the glass edges
Of our dining car & shine on metal things.

You would open the pantry door
& there it was—luminating
Like the wherewithal of every important song
Ever written. We never moved on, went on
Living in our lot like a box of wild chives
That refused to die off.

The night I met you in the kite field
It was spring & you wanted to be flying.
This was what you wanted all along
To steer by star, to talk into the air soft
As a sixteen-year-old girl.
You were full of the kinds of truths
That only bad boys think they know.
I have always been a liar.

Now you're gone too & that's one more
Of us who won't go ragging into old age.
Before you died, you confessed
In violence that you would have this piece
Of everlasting life. Any fool
Can see that you are gone for good.
I'm learning to be quiet
Like a good passenger.

Magnum Mysterium

Since I've lived in many places, it's odd
That I continue to waken in Nebraska,
Wandering into the sunroom where the wheat
Has come up wide overnight.

If I lived in a railroad car,
I could keep an eye on the weather,
The clouds a gallery of passing obsessions.
I could fathom things that way.

I could watch heat subsume the corn
& in winter watch the quarries
Churning great chunks of marble,
Feel how cold it really is.

If I have some important thing to say
I hope I live here long enough
To say it gracefully. The wind moves
Everything. Nothing is exempt.

In the space between seasons
Which is one night in a life,
The corn beats inside its stalks, waiting for bloom.
The wheat flowers, falls easily.
The clouds become enormous & have names.

Autobiography

It is only three o'clock & already I'm alone
Listening to the lovers next door
Like Patsy Cline & her Man
Throwing barebacked wooden furniture
Like the real life bicker of true love.
I love that hands-on,
Die-while-you're-dark-haired-still
& young, fists curled to desire,
Take Me kind of love.
They'll make love without apology
& I'll be left to the afternoon
& the autoerotic sounds of my American voice
Getting it all down.

October Seventh, Nineteen Eighty-Three

When everything seems a message,
A small cue of light beneath the door,
Shadows that move too early
When the thing which they are mimicking
Is still, the car crash at Lochlyn
In the middle of the dawn
& no survivors anywhere in sight.

Not that I don't have the same chemicals
That everyone else has too.
It isn't that I am alone
Or that my certain breed
Of bliss catches fire in the wrong
Times & I'm bewildered with a joy
So large I could expire.

Tonight is my ten thousandth night.
It happens in the middle of my twenty-seventh
Year. I am one-third done with this.
It happens suddenly, without warning, like the loss
Of signal lanterns in electric storms,
Like a wound appearing out of nowhere
Where before there was clean flesh.

I kept hearing about the Underground
In reckless cities all over the world,
How important danger will become in a tunnel
Situation. How caution means nothing,
How the music of traveling too fast
Has everything to do with risk & melancholia.
I am drawn to figments & occasion:

REM sleep, Winter Solstice, the Blind Man's
Afternoons. I would read for him
In a Cambrian room which smelled of dread
& dance there for him barefoot
On a black rug, as if he could see
The color of the inside of my mouth
From a room six thousand miles away.

October Seventh, Nineteen Eighty-Three

I have come to this. Those of us whose eyes
By chance, genetics, aptitude, go down
On the ends will be perceived as perpetually sad.
There is nothing quite exact to fear
& these are hours of exactitude.

As if it would be possible to live
In random increments or know
That no one knows which thing
Will happen next. This many days
Into my life, I have come to this.

October, I am in possession of my name.
Sorcerer, this is substantial life we're speaking of.
Light, you loom upon these days
As if everything has its certain purpose
Like an inebriated monk illuminating a great text.

The Future as a Cow

> *I can't say the future is not a cow.*
> *The cow may be my future. I don't know.*
>
> MANUTE BOL

From the great warm side of the animal
heaving with meat, as she breathes out
the day tightens to this rare night.

The herds put their faces as close to the ground
as possible, listening for what grows
& moves, for what is kind, the stuff
of this dark earth, clean as the day
before this day, we were the only ones alive
preparing for the news of some momentous thing.

I like this world like no one
else has ever liked this world.
I can't say there isn't a certain
amount of radioactivity. I can't say
anyone will save anyone

because I know
by now about cherishing & miraculous deaths
& the deep days of summer which lie
ahead of us & I might know
what is lost

as the girls in North Dakota waken in the midst
of their own blonde hair & tie it back
with grosgrain, startled somewhere in the middle
of this landlocked dream, or that they had dreamt
of anything other than bliss,
one you can know, but never have.

That what is lost
cannot be gotten back.

& the animals move together
bunching,
grazing their softest parts
against the ground, each other,
most vulnerable of all.

I took care of the cows. I looked for animals
which would like to kill the cows.
Sometimes I talk out loud to keep them away.

Edward VI on the Seventh Day

I

Father is a large man
he has what I have not yet known
a passion, he has greatness in his gowns
& all of England at his beck & call.
I know when he is walking how I love
to hear the airs about him echo
in the halls are great & frigid as his foot
steps hard & harrowing come toward my room
& here I wait for him, he is superior.

II

His robes are deep with steam
& blue, he rarely touches me.
But listens by each morning from the door's
bold other wooden side, my voice is high
he listens as I sing my lessons louder
when I hear the footsteps stop
his breath is big, I want so much to please
him, then he bursts inside to see me
small blue boy, a version miniature
stand shortly on a velvet chair, recite
the Classics, beaming. But I never smile
near him, must not laugh.
I will be him someday.

III

I am, by far, too fair for him.
He is dark & brilliant with a temper, fire
I am airy, scampering. The ladies say
that I am frail, my fingers womanish.
He doesn't know me, know that I am quite
so small & elegant as this.
It is a son, October
when he bellowed & the corridors
went marbled with a blaze & heat

& it was I, small thing, that made him bellow
when my mother died it was: a son.
I will learn to move the air about me widely
as he does, an animal as wild & vile with scent
a face as terrible & bearded, hands
as loud & difficult as his, as passionate.

IV

A blue night in November when we stood
outside together with the owls & hounds
all bothered by the first chill evening howling
when our breath made muted billowings of talk
the things he told me made some ice upon his whiskers
& he is quite excitable when he is cold I think.
He told me what is power & he told me why
I must grow tall, he told me when to set the bells
in motion for a death or for the sake of bliss
he said, or for a hunger, for a woman.
He told me how to dance he told me everything.

V

The first time that I set the bells
in motion will be morning.
By the light of day, a season changing
one to two & tolling two to one
that much the smaller then to none.
White winter & in January I am him.

VI
& all of England at my beckoned call.

Edward VI on the Seventh Day

VII

Earth it is the last grey winter all consumed
the lack of angles & the smoothness watered
of a child's face. I was to be a man by now
& heralding the pierce green matters of the spring.
By evening I am thin & underripe
as pale as masks all meant for ghosts
& things of underground all spirited
& newborn in their vapoured states.
He told me then
he told me everything
I've never danced
& now these humours all confused:
black bile, blood & I am chilled the bells
are counting hours like the years of me
not happened yet, too many hours as the bells
are moving wind about them, hallowing & huge
& passing once then twice now past the midnight
I am fevered I am pretty
in a plague of white & bells
are calling out the days & seasons
in Westminster Abbey, vaulting
& the bells are coughing
I was of my father I am King.

(T W O)

Jessica, from the Well

I

This is what it was like: the morning
pale all above me, a patch of sky
like a blue poker flung into a floor
of earth, this is what I have to go on.
I am on my knees at first, a Jessica
a prayer—I pray against the rose
caliche, the hardpan rock, a marbling
of new wound in my forehead.
I've never spoken aloud yet to anyone
alive, but I know all the words.

On Wednesday morning I slipped down
the shaft like the small mythic creature
I have always known I ought to be.
No one was looking.
I am mutable still, I fold myself.
It is a gift to be this small & aboriginal.
Even without food, I am growing
& I find this frightful that my body
will become too large to live here comfortably.
The earth opens for me
as I always knew it would for a wish.

II

All day, I am divined
by sunlight & October has gone
damask, ocherous. When I learn a word
sometimes, I am compelled to use it.
Given my disposition, I will always be
circuitous, precocious, an Embellisher.
Like Oskar, I can make a world
change with my voice, can shatter the diamond
tipped bits of the drill, can make the wells' walls glitter
back at me. My own voice travels sideways
as it zigzags to the titian center
of the earth & curls back up to me

Jessica, from the Well

like a seamstress' needle against her thimble
in the very center of the Taj Mahal.
I am the only one alive.

By dusk, I am running out
of ways to warm myself.
I have warmed my self with my self.
My own limbs curled all about me, fetal.
Sometimes, I am so obvious like that.
I sing & somewhere above, they can hear me
humming along with myself & myself.
A choir of me's.
By nightfall, only a small albino fracture
will be left of the moon
& I will have lost all light to navigate.
Soon I will be famous.

III

By midnight, I can hear my own heart thump
against the well, dry for a million miles
till it hits the water corrugated by the beating
as it ripples back to me. It is instantly
recognizable, the way a mother cat knows
her own by scent & self love. It is me.
Before this day, my skin was never marred
& Quaker pink. My forehead has opened now
quite by happenstance, the etching on a wall
of an undiscovered cave, unlucky hieroglyph.

Take, for instance, my right leg
which, by midnight, I have accidentally wedged
in a notorious & irredeemable position.
I hate to be unnatural, especially in personal geometry
& by now, the leg has lodged irrevocably up
against my face, unbound, unfortunate.
There is to be no turning
back & I will sing & think of crying
for the first time so they'll know
at last I've blundered. I lean

into the rock, a willful child, a little bruised
& if I go out I will die dreaming.

I V

I had forgotten the small news of the night
between dreams & waking into the warm
smooth blown air shimmying down the oval
of the well. In the whole history of song
I know very few. So this is what it's like.
I am fixing on the hemp clothesline
strung across Aunt Jamie Moore's backyard,
on last week's laundered sheets, triangled
like sails, splashed with hyacinth & vetch
they stiffen in the wind against a Texan cobalt
sky. It is dawn. All night long
my eyes widened to accommodate the lack
of light, a self-illumined glowfish flat
on its side, I keep my flicker constant, wide awake
while sleeping, both eyes ajar.

Big gangly weepy gamey men, Sweethearts & Insomniacs,
keep prodding me   *to sing.*
And I sing.

And: *Move your foot for me, Juicy.*
And I wiggle it back for the man.

And: *How does a kitten go?*
And I go like a kitten goes, on

& on in that throaty liquid lewd bowlegged
voice like kittens make.
Then shut these big ole eyes.

V

Someday, I will be buried above ground
like Monroe, vaulted
always in the midst of flowers & sentiment.
On the descent, I was magically compact
boneless, as agile as water itself always

Jessica, from the Well

on the way toward other water.
The noise of my own form against the loosening
walls as I am born into the dark
rococo teratogenic rooms of the underground.
All the noise of the world
stops here & muffles, muffles me.
This town knows how to drill.
Sometimes my imagination gets to running wild.

Bring me back
alive. It was so simple to come down.
I wake with my own hair wound
into my fist, in sleep I've torn my own
self   —*pretty, milky curls.*
A spool of me.
In the matter of my toes, there has been damage done
but when I come back, they'll pinken up I'm sure.
In America: *Hard Work & Prayer.*
Resilience is bliss in the body,
the voodoo of immunity,
the will to come back,
Deliverance.

V I

Surrounded by jelly, an accoutrement of eros for ascent
from the well, I am born.
Wide eyed & swaddled in white linens, I emerge
pristine & preserved, like some Egyptian form
accompanied & gifted
with all the Nilotic charms
necessary for the long quicksilver moments
of the Afterlife.
So this is it.
I rub my eyes in newslight as if awakening
from the mere corn yellow husks
of slumber of an ordinary lateday nap.

The heart is left   *in situ,* I am lifted
from the oubliette

divine by water, blinking by air.
I cannot speak a word yet, but I know them all.
I sing, holding a piece of myself in my hand,
it is hair & fear & the church bells muscle
against each other
& the earth opens for me
as I always knew it would for a myth.
Given my character, I will always be mercurial,
a little sentimental, star-shaped & terrestrial
divine by water, healed by air
luminescent, inconceivable, a prayer
a Jessica,   *I sing.*

Hitchcock Blue

These we take for granted:
The blue turn of the water at Three.
The bones of the lover alone
Still life in Prussian blue.
The blonde in the fur cap
At the northern seaport in late November.
These given which we have come to regard:
Anima, Animus

I have gone into the fire & lived
There. I told you in a letter
You touch it only once, you watch it
For awhile you enter the flame.
The blue part of the scald, the part
That mars the skin, remembering
It will not forgive, forever.
That's a pretty thing.

We imagined life without that auburn heat
Of the south, ultra marine by day, direct.
Aniline & dangerous by dusk, midnight
Blue by midnight as we lay together in that blue
Of blues we said the soul, a girl, could travel
Anywhere, could read the hieroglyphs
Could dream the cornflowers out of nothingness
Could weather any temperature or fire
Bombing, could watch the death of any small
Thing we were metaphysical
When we were young like that.

Imagine this: that it is summer
In the Arctic Regions now. That all the ice
Has come down washing the earth clean
Of its hands. Even if I were alive
Then & loose in Dresden as a little girl
Even if I had lived through that winter
& come to the west to watch you
In white as you did your alchemies,
Even then I would want you as some
Thing I could write down, some palpable
Milori blue substance, a metal, a stone.

Kid Flash

Born in the dark, you come back up,
it's a red thing, nightclubbing.
Once, in the Cat's Paw
I fell in love with each man at the bar,
their deeply flanneled arms, their slow bond
with other boys, their back roads,
the women they would never share.

I hate the day coming back
like the horn with its mute inside.
I hate the sheets suspect of tousling
by some other two,
the clothes that seem dampened
by some bygone decade
when you smooth them back on.

Into jazz which makes no children,
into the high wind of the boardwalk,
the aristocracy of a girl's free afternoons,
into the south of boys traveling,
the stucco motel with two-hour coupling shifts,
into the north of men drinking clear
water, to the cafe in New York
where the horn player is always hungry
sweaty, lit in red & you
backing him up, me
in the diamondback dawn, needing
all new clothes, born
in the early morning heat, back up
from camp, I think
I was lonely for everyone in the world.

Heartbeat

Let me be brief then
I will go on worshiping
the perfect mean lines, the light
on them visible only through the neon
signs of life, the parts which glow
all night when peaceful sorts are sleeping,
when the wanderers are still avenging
their insomnia in the dark
false hellebore red of poolhalls,
in the allnight pastel caves of laundromats,
in the wrong decade coffee shop in Ypsilanti
where even the manager can't lend the key
to the men's room,
                            I love
these things too, the self serve
filling station where a pale hand
sneaks out making silver
change, or the one dark palm
in the meat shop on Amsterdam & 110th
behind the curtain handing out
the little envelopes of *Heartbeat,*
                            I covet
these things too,
some third world after this one
& the one that goes hereafter,
in that world you will be important,
devoured by the fawns,
inscrutable Christmas rose, toxic
in your leather coat phase for a long time
worshiping the long blonde stains left
after light & after fire.

Archaeology

A girl goes to the mountains every day
Unearthing dawn after dawn, wishing
The sifting bones would rise to the top

Like the separate castes of cream, white,
Whiter, the most white. She will bring home
The pieces of an old world, line them gentle,

Side by side on the woolly Aztec blanket
On her bed. The ashblonde ivory of the tooth,
The one lost rib, the armour of the good hollow

Skull, the long musical speech of the spine
Penultimate to the starstricken glory of the tail,
The tiny symmetry of chambers in the conch shell

Of the inner ear, the dark red gloom of the pelvic
Arc, two withered fingers in their curl.
You, born walking on this earth, accidental

American thing, wound in this rock bed gorge,
Watched wordlessly as the ice washed over
You till the world was frozen & waited

For the girl to find you there, startled, curled
Into the same dream you were dreaming
In your own jade youth. Then she will have you

Now & need to know: *What was it like?*
You will answer, monumental dreamer.
She will ask again & you will answer.

The Letter L

Someday I won't feel things anymore.
In the false light of a hotel room

Where the sheets will be old, worn
Into a perpetual softness by strangers,

A grim moon catches in the boughs
Of the old lamp by the bed,

I am your apprentice. I look for the L
In my name in places of light, lucky,

The good ending of tenderly. The psychic
Leaves the past, sand covers Egypt,

Moves constantly to arrive at the streak
Of the yet-to-be. It's quirky, this grace

Of telling, the low moonlight of an odd
Decade all over the linoleum floor.

He smells light souring
Cream, something wrong.

Near the harbor where the little lights
Will be strung up for the solstice,

When it's time, I will look there
For your name. You have taught me

To look for lies in relics,
Jewels, flaws. I come home

& someone's always in the back seat
Of my car, wailing for Ray Charles,

Left handed, one window left lit
In a small town full of dark trailers,

Late winter, last of the 1900's.
Someone is still awake.

Playing Havoc

So another one has walkd
into the sea and left something
worn on a black rock,
it's the legacy of costume left
after stars get dark & die.

I am thinking of you in a nickel city
in Ohio, ready to blow off. Your finger hookd
around the implement that cuts thin glass,
on the C-note key of your alto saxophone,
the curld gesture of   *Come Here.*

About your innocence, I am unsure.
Someday you will kill off
a luminous star.
So another blue ruin
of a figure in a raincoat

slips into the streetscape, coverd
with history, mist, back turnd, a little
deadly. Our brief generation
hasn't even yet begun descent
early bloomer, I'm coming home.

Danse Macabre

What the sailors thought on that last night
As they fell in little heaps on the deck

Asleep beneath the scythes
Of the Norwegian stars, adrift

Until six hundred years from now, their ship
Will sail back home, still with its cargo full
Of sheep's wool, accidents, the semi-precious
Spices of an Asian girl who ran away.

As if you wanted now to tell me after all
This time what Giovanni was about to say
At five o'clock on a Friday afternoon
As he wrote down his last Italian majuscule

In the rushlight of a sun gone
Rancid with indifference & fell

To a summer night when even the moon
Was a sickle of fire & a whole city kicked off
Its covers in the heat, on a night when bad dreams
Were invented & you gave in. Imagine this:

The last friar in the north of France, latching
The door to his room, leaving his shoes by the bed,
Writing it all down so you would know
Exactly what it is to trick oblivion.

What were you thinking as the ripe wheat stood
Uncut in fields, the peasants bundled in the streets,
The Pope preserved between two blazing fires,
When even the boldest wolves retreated to dark,

When night letters were sent
& never arrived, burning to speak?

What the Whales Sound Like
in Manhattan

There had been some small confusion, some
commotion on the upper reaches of this island,
on the West Side where the sun was setting

like the reigns of emperors gone obsolete.
It was a sunset of a certain alchemy
of oranges with the blues of bruises healing.

It was where the river smell was slightly rancid,
slightly salted, slightly breathless & aroused.
There had been some wonderful confoundment

on the Avenue of the Americas, something
blocking buses & pedestrians. It was something
unemployed & elegant, it was a whale come home

for night. In Manhattan what the whales
sound like at night is blue & unpossessable.
This sound is something only they can do.

It is a sound that catches on the canopies
of pre-war highrise buildings designed to keep out
light & Latin music & the seeds of Chinese children

eating kiwis on these handsome summer nights.
It is a sound that tips the gryphons on the tops
of buildings, one that spreads the concrete wings

of gargoyles clutched to rooftops looking out
for seasons. In Manhattan it is not that common
to have whales. Bowing west, the Ming Men

take home their tangerines & porcelains.
Vehicles have learned to pass the thing
on Broadway, headlights bruise its hide.

What the Whales Sound Like in Manhattan

The animal is spent & cares no longer
if the taxis honk or merchants or late travelers
take pokes at it. The stoplight changes red

to green resounding on the whale's great
shimmered rind. As an emperor folds
his napkin at the last meal of his dynasty,

luminous & moribund, inside the whale
the sound is one tympanic archaeology.
The bones are perfect as the gospel wind.

The Beginning of the Beginning

At dawn they are beginning
The small fires around my home.
I am afraid of what the world will do.
They huddle at the fires warming
Their hands, pawing the heat.
I long to come that close to flame.
As the sun spills out

This first extinct red light
I watch them from my window, watch
Them worship something warmer,
Much more powerful than I could ever be.
I am waiting for the season to give in.
I do not believe in punishment.
The world will rise by morning red

At the tips of its wings.
What the world will do it will keep
On doing. By day, I will be light again.
I will survive & outsurvive the hours.
I will have done wrong in my sleep.
I will have dreamed of fires warmer
Fires smaller, much more beautiful.
Far more hungry, worshiped, singed.

In a Landlocked Time

There is nothing like the mistral lull
of fishermen devoting days to the sea.
That is the kind of love which I require,
the forty years of worship for the weather,
the homage to the captured thing.

A year ago, I was preparing my body.
A scouring, the long oiled baths, the embalming
with fragrances & color, my long love of ritual.
When all else fails, you see me resorting to mythologies
& I become the Hyperborean that I am.

As of yesterday, it was irrevocably fall.
There was to be no turning back,
we were deep into it then. I am attendant
on this time the time between
the north wind & the present tense.

The landlord had tied down the trees, wrapping
their roots in canvas cloths. He put out
offerings, the bucketfuls of sand left
at the top & bottom of each set of stairs.
Even the salt air could not undo the ice.

He was preparing us for storm.
He was preparing for a time
when the lights would burn even by day.
In this small town, by winter
when only the warmblooded were left,

the fishermen could call out
of hypnosis the water-breathing
creatures which were slowing in the middle
of their tracks, their long descent
into a winter's night.

I am a creature of the real world, even
though you think I seldom choose to live there
properly. I am an air-breathing sort:
always cold at the extremity, never content
with the heat that I have.

In a Landlocked Time

A year ago, I was waterproofing myself
in virgin wool for the cold ride out
to watch the whales as they waited
for winter & hesitated, not too far
from land.   In a landlocked time

I have never seen their great grey backs bending
the surface of the sea, never seen their cool reluctance
to stray too far from human warmth.

Lucie & Her Sisters

It's not enough to have my one dream in hand long after I am gone. I'll be a locust by then, learning in the next life how to fly transparently, how to deposit my old skins on the outside of the screened-in porch in some pastoral set in the last open space in America a hundred years from now. For now, I am transfixed by possessing the things of this world.

The littlest sister phones collect. She's run away from home, the first child in our family to be slapped in the face. She sleeps her first night in the Victoria House. She's too young to have a calling yet. Bells toll, the noon whistle passes over the town, over the phone like emergency, a slate cloud. Fishermen feel it on the bay. Lobsters stir in their crates. It is almost spring. She's seventeen. She says the town is like a stage set being torn down, a play that's had its run.

Sometimes I think the world's coming to end. Joel called this morning on his way to Halifax. His mother has a rare deterioration of the eye. She's losing the middle of everything. I imagine that she sees him as a mane of dark Polynesian hair, no features left. She lived her life in books, he says. Now she reads the white outside aisles of each page. She watches television through a round glass bauble, listens. They pick our softest parts to take away.

The oldest sister phones at the orchid hour of Southern California Time. By the time our father dies, we will learn to guard each other, vigilant. For one November day, we lived together in his glass home, built above our coal, at the crack of the highest hill of *Gan Aden,* a cove farm. An opulence in Ruff Creek, a miner's town, a bowl herd of Black Angus silhouettes, invisible by evening. Our mineral rights, curled in a humpbacked trunk in someone else's wooden attic, were never found. Someday, we will inherit each other. She will have her life in her hands.

A middle sister calls from Washington. She has a secret, governmental. It's too dark to speak of. The whole family could wind up back in Pittsburgh with an investigator parked in our driveway, surveying us, making his move to come in, to question us, to find out if any of us have ever lied. We have, all of us. It's too soon to tell.

I don't want to be around to watch them die. Tonight, one of us sleeps in the Victoria, old angels guard the wooden bed. The air in seatowns never has a chance to dry. Things moult. Everything is old. The mail is damp & old. I don't want to be around to watch a family dying off. I want to be the first.

Each plague species exists in two phases: solitary & gregarious. Bands of nymphs wander & adult swarms take flight spontaneously on warm days like these when the body temperature is high.

Two thousand square miles of green-veined wings, we cross the Atlantic & some get lost along the way as the cool air of nights at sea catches in our own wind, the wind we make when we possess everything in our paths in order to survive & feed. In a new century, I will be in solitary phase, dislocated from the swarm on a flight from the desert in West Africa to the New World.

There on the outside of the screened-in porch, I will cling, feeling smug but slightly maudlin regarding the publication of my collected work. It is nearly night. The dark beasts are grazing, digesting constantly, switching their tails back & forth in the faint wheeze of the warm air. A northern wind rustles in the meadow grass. Dogs bark because they always do in pastorals, answering each other like the wolves they once were in another life.

Sometimes, my heart beats too fast for its own folds. I am this, genetically. Ann sleeps the deep sleep of the near-redeemed; she has no veil to speak of. Julie sleeps easily with secrets; she wishes on anything, anything. Melissa sleeps near the sea because she thinks that, once, I was saved there, born into the damp air of an old desire to stay alive for anything, at all costs. I hear the weather coming on. I wake all night & listen to my neighbor's yard fill up with the metallic sound of snow in early spring. A globe of light comes on in their attic & some nights, you could swear that it's the moon. It's dark there, that dark. You can be easily deceived.

(T H R E E)

Elective Mutes

Nobody suffers the way I do. Not with a sister . . .
But this sister of mine, a dark shadow robbing me
of sunlight, is my one and only torment.

JUNE GIBBONS

Tuesday afternoon, Broadmoor

I

In summertime, when we were little, I remember we
walking with synchronized steps, a four-armed girl,
we've got everything
the same. We were eleven, a shadow & a shadow
of her shadow. I am born
first & I teach my sister to be quiet.
Here's the secret:
One day we will burn buildings together.
One day we will set fire to great things.
It sends shudders down my spine.
In the heat of swing park, we will take boys
down & mingle with them in the brushes.
In a basket, we will float down rivers, Venus
rising infrared, you've no idea
what it's like to have this other
half. We floating like hot house
fuchsia, two Chinese lanterns
through the water edge, a bulrush, shooting
stars. I will teach you to be perfect, more
quiet. I will teach you to be hard high self
mutilating. We will talk patois, speeded
up 78 on the record player, so no one else
can understand. We do, we know
the languages of hemlock, jimson weed.
Sometimes, my hands smell like sex.
That summer if anyone looked at one of us
we froze, like girls made of bloodstone,
crackleware. We kiln things.
We love each other like we grew
from the same set of pelvic bone,

Elective Mutes

as if we were attached like clethra
flowers to their stems.
We're budding now.

I I

We were sixteen & took to our room.
J & I are two coloured girls of history.
We do dolls, most are twinnies like we are.
I am the vicar here, the dolls marry
on the floor, kneeling on a red patch
of my mother's velvet dress.
We sing hymns we stain the hymnsheets
in the colours of medieval luminations
the colour of Mars, some nights bloodred,
the blue of Mercury, azury
like the sky lit up all over America,
a clear suburban summer
night & the lawnmower's stopped
& the swimming pools are filled up
with the bice of night
water, a town in mid-America gone
mad, deserted. Someday we'll live there
when everyone's gone to the drive-in
& blonde twins are on the roofs of cars
or lounging on their sunchairs in the dark, soaking
up their moon, all the convertible tops
are down & the speakerbox hangs
on the rear view mirror like a locust,
slow & distorted like that
& you climb in back to have a boy
inside you, that's what I want, on the back seat
sprawling in the noises like an animal
he makes, but you're shy, you're bourgeois, you talk
American which I sort of like but it's kind of sleazy, you know?
But me & Jennifer are up here in our room, broadcasting
Radio Gibbons in the gloom of an English outpost of the RAF.
These are my children now.

FROM THE REGISTER OF DEATHS OF DOLLS:

> *June Gibbons. Aged 9. Died of leg injury.*
> *George Gibbons. Aged 4. Died of eczema.*
> *Bluey Gibbons. Aged two and a half. Died of appendix*
> *Peter Gibbons. Aged 5. Adopted. Presumed dead.*
> *Polly Morgan-Gibbons. Age 4. Died of a slit face*
> *Susie Pope-Gibbons died the same time of a cracked skull.*

We forecast the weather from our room.

III

Dear Lord, you have no idea
what it was like.   *11 June, 1981.*
I want a baby of my own, caged wren, tiny
trapped inside me like a blow of laurel
growing in a field, high & taking
from my own blood like an other only smaller,
someone I can call my own.
We to Welsh Hook & down into the barn.
J's lover, Carl, is there he *broke*
my virginity tonight. She
watched us, there was we
& blackeyed broken glass fallen
from the windows & a wild bird caught up
in the rafters, couldn't find his way back out.
Shrike: hangs its prey on wire fences, thorns.
This is what it felt like: for the first time
now I am alive. We did it
to the Stylistics, J watching
then we lay down heavy in the hay, heat
sticking stalks up under my blouse,
strawflowers, a resurrection weed inside of me.
Smoke: indicates confusion.
Fire: desire for escape.
Shoes off, summer night, whole world
smells of fennel, all romance
from the Book of Red Dreams:
Arson: indicates a twining.
Bitch: flammable, a lover.

Elective Mutes

Nakedness: perfection, fire inside thing consumed.
Sometimes we even dream the same, get that.

I burned it down today.

I V

Without my shadow, would I die?
At school once, in a tuberculosis scare
when we uncurled our limbs for vaccination
ours were the only coloured arms.
Pink pink pink pink black. I love
flowers. When we grow wild we are.
No one can hear us talk, we mute we shy.
The other girls are none of we.

From   *The Little Books for Little Angels:*

It is Christmas Day. The TV's on all afternoon. Lassie, Bo-
nanza, imports from America. It is ten years ago, I have this
dream. There are five children, blue-eyed little angels. There's
a bird on top our tree. The TV's gone blue, all the stars of the
show are Twinnies. My father in his big old resting chair.
Everyone's dressed in Victorian clothes, as if there's been a
wedding. White gloves & something catches fire. J is on her
knees. We've come home from putting flowers on our moth-
er's grave. She isn't really dead yet, she feeds us bloodpudding
for supper. Everyone talking with no vowels. It's snowing
hard & our house is getting more & more muffled. I've blue
eyes, covered with lace. J & I are brides. We both have this
disease of the lung. We are inseparable.

We'll die early & be stars.

V

By the next summer, we'd bandaged our breasts
down so hard we could barely breathe.
High on vodka & glue, we both fuck the same

boy. Lupine, hawthorne, love-lies-bleeding,
small violence of scent.
Something like magic is happening.
You've no idea how much I am
she. I am she. *Dear Lord,*
I am scared of her. She is not normal.
Someone is driving her insane. It is me.
Tonight she wound a cord around my neck
to strangle me, *6 November, Furzy Park.*
She broke our ritual, she goes too far.
We take brandy from beneath our bed,
go to Gipsy Lane to walk.
Wolfbane, daphne, trillium.
Really it's more of debris
there than anything else, the river's drying up.
But tonight, everything is full.
It has been raining for days.
Everything is dripping
like pen & ink drawings, long & lean
as the blackened Modigliani faces of my sister's art.
We entice each other constantly
in these beautiful nights
after neverending rain—
    First of all, I wept to God
—when world is wet & shy, under the bridge, I hold her
head down under
water & I feel her thrash
against me, just this once, I murder her,
it's a once in a lifetime thing you know?
You have no idea
how much I love her, I am she.
Sweet alyssum, larkspur, yew.
We kiss. Monkshood, nasturtium,
forget me not.

I Wish You Love

Like Josef's skull ascending from Brazilian soil
On a twine, she rises from her famous white bed,
Exhumed by morning. I am hunted into daylight
When I wake like that, god-hungry, startled.
Now that my father is gone, he has gone
Luminous. *I wish him love.*

The late sun comes to my own midwestern heart
At evening. Nights now, the anorexic soul
In spandex tights slips out of bed with me,
Spreads her black acrylic legs, tendons
The color of an unreasonably aroused male animal,
Starving, always wide & wide awake.

I want movie kinds of kisses. Now Dietrich's dead,
I'm ankle-deep in melancholia again.
A man & his little girl on a stamen red sleigh, first
Snowfall of the year, both oddly blonde in the bare
Afternoon, downhill. In the matter of the breaking
Of the heart, we are easily fractured. *I wish you shelter*

From the storm, A cozy fire to keep you warm.
I knew it would feel this way. I never knew
It would feel like this. A man in an English stadium
Caught in a wintry patch of flame, rolls down the green
Of Yorkshire, begging for water, longing to be put out
Like a pinched wick, snuffed, an old horse gone lame.

This morning, half of the Rhine was declared biologically dead.
By nightfall, the eels will be floating face up toward Germany,
Lighthearted & unlovely. I will wait for you in Schaffhausen.
There's a puncture in the southern reaches
Of the earth's protective atmosphere. I'm trying
To be moved by this, but I'm more piqued by Rapture now.

No one will ever love you like you wanted to be loved.
Your new woman is Easy on the Eye, you say. Since this recent
Nomenclature for the Wind Chill, the world's a colder place
I think. Less than zero Tuesday night.
I'm the kind of girl who calls from baths in old extravagant hotels.
I think of ruined thighs. *I wish you bluebirds in the spring.*

I was drinking moonshine out of a clear cup. You Montana
Boys will marry one day after all, in small vehicular domiciles.
Nothing changes much. The stupor of these cold November nights,
A wife stewing gumbos in a crockpot. I will travel east to New Jersey,
Land of the Most Lovely. Even the dead want to go home.
Someone made them promises they couldn't keep. *My loving heart*

& I agree, Now is the time to set you free. When I got off
The tracks of a long afternoon into this turnip-colored earth,
You were drunk & down somewhere in America, your father in the deep
South, courting a girl still in a cotton frock this late in the year.
When my own father died, we buried him with a trout fisher's book
& we all thought we couldn't go on anymore. I can't take my eyes

Off the news. Planes pass constantly over the snow belt,
Even in peacetime & the roads here go on & on, unreasonably flat.
No one is baptized. After a death in the family
Gadgets go wrong for awhile; it's nothing
You shouldn't expect, the near-collapse of anything electrical
Or bound by heat or light. This is the gospel truth.

In the evangelic dusk
Way past the Bible belt, they're killing off
Large common beasts, shackle & hoist method.
Don't you think they know what's going on?
All of those old prophets were the same: doom, doom.
But most of all, When snowflakes fall

I wish you love. Monday, after a long weekend, your sister woke
Tattooed. Small, softtalking at the hip, coming for to carry her home.
These things aren't revocable, you know; it's a graceful, toxic kind
Of thing, tattoos. *I wish her love.* I miss my man again,
Curious & passionate like Josef's bones arising after all these years
Alone & unidentified in South America. I bid this slim farewell.

Now Dietrich's dead; we turn left here.

Ten Years Apprenticeship in Fantasy

My Darling C,

There is something to be said for Nature after all, dusk pending, variable stars. I have had a change in luminosity.

All winter long, I've tried not to write to you. There is something too final to it I should think. First, news of America: the farmers are being winnowed out again. Now that I have cable television, I am in touch with the world. In the rain last night, rice went for twenty-five cents a pound in the midwest. Blacks lined the barnlike edges of their city, umbrellaed by eaves & politics & the fair price of near-proteins. I, myself, as you know, have been starving alternately for a decade. Everyone wants to know why & I tell them it's my way of holding the world back.

Also, on the evening news, I saw a six-legged steer. The father (his master) reports that Beauty is in the Eye of the Beholder. He loves that thing. Everyone wants to know how many hearts it has. Only one.

In the more immediate vicinity of my house where—you should know, it is just on the verge of twilight—I have courted this darkness lying face down into my hands all afternoon, absolutely loathing the light, doing Gestalt fantasies (you're allowed, I hear, to feel healthy in erotic dreams of submission), waiting for an orange moon to bloom into the nightsky, waiting for absolute quiet, waiting to get vulnerable again.

Where I used to live, the fog slid off the great bourbon-colored mountain to roost around my house at dawn. It was as thick as a religious cough. Here, cats come down the corridors of the city streets like the selected survived. No one is rich anymore. The extended family makes its comeback in the clapboard houses where all porch-sitting has been suspended until spring.

There's a big to-do about lymphocytes & immunities, what with all of us living so close together, the quick, violent, unapproachable deaths of so many of us here. The body's weather allows each germ to enter musically: ethereal, fullblown. Of lymphocytes, I imagine they are one-celled stars in the big liquid chambers of the body underwater: glowing & attentive, lighting the way as they linger in that great invertebrate chain of hankering.

I know you get depressed when I get all lofty like this. I've been reading the Romantics since two o'clock. Even the poets married. I find comfort in this fact, though it besieges me with awe. Those of us who are susceptible to weather might be marred by the great heaving effort of the winter as it turns.

As I approach evening I wait for the sound of stars crackling. I have never heard this noise, not yet. I imagine it is never cool there in the long, bright, monolithic hour of each star. It tickles me, actually, that this light received expired long before I ever spoke. Like this letter, which, if passed from hand to hand, will reach you long after I am gone. This moment will continue for as long as you imagine / *Me. Until the star goes blank & quivers / Until it becomes vividly cold / Possessed by an old / Gravity & falls.*

In closing, let me remind you of the Siamese twins separated not long ago in Canada. They let the little one, the concave half, be girl. Without her, he will skip quicker, eat more heartily, raise up his own kind & I think he should be given that one good chance. What better reason to go on living than to repeat yourself autobiographically? She didn't have that chance you understand.

I know the storm has reached past your knees by now & the electricity falters & the mail has become erratic & you're living on your thoughtful supply of canned goods. Don't let your teeth & hair get weak, as certain vitamins & minerals are missed sorely in a bland diet of single-minded sustenance. Pray only that the heat inside lasts until this thing has passed. Stay up all night if you have to, to avoid bad dreaming. It can hurt you & I need you. I am, as ever, yours.

And So Long, I've Had You Fame

How odd that she would die into an August
night, I would have thought
she would have gone out in a pale clear
night of autumn, covered to the shoulder
in an ivory sheet, hair
fanned out across the pillow perfectly.
Fame will go by, and, so long, I've had you, Fame.
From under the door, the lights leak
into the hall & Sinatra going
over & over in the bedroom on repeat.
I was six & you were dying out.
I was sitting in a sky blue metal chair
in our kitchen in the east
digesting the fact, still, of my mother's second
honeymoon & the man living all over
our house, that she loved him, had him hard.
The sun was on our kitchen table, lighting
the back of my hand & the headline
in the *Post Gazette* said you were done.
That you were dying
even in the hour when our neighborhood
went indigo last night, in the hour
when our palms were stained by Sno-Cones,
in the hour when Russell's father would take home
the bases from the baseball diamond,
then my sister & I would move like spiders
into the nests of our dotted swiss nightgowns,
in the hours of a windless August night
in Pittsburgh & somewhere
Sinatra redundant
no one lifts the needle up, he's singing
like an angel
all night long along the famous dusk
of the Pacific shoreline
as your breathing slowed into the sweetest
toxic nothingness, so long, I've had you, face
down,   *Cursum Perficio.*

After the Grand Perhaps

After vespers, after the first snow
has fallen to its squalls, after New Wave,
after the anorexics have curled
into their geometric forms,
after the man with the apparition
in his one bad eye has done red things
behind the curtain of the lid & sleeps,
after the fallout shelter in the elementary school
has been packed with tins & other tangibles,
after the barn boys have woken, startled
by foxes & fire, warm in their hay, every part
of them blithe & smooth & touchable,
after the little vandals have tilted
toward the impossible seduction
to smash glass in the dark, getting away
with the most lethal pieces, leaving
the shards which travel most easily
through flesh as message
on the bathroom floor, the parking lots,
the irresistible debris of the neighbor's yard
where he's been constructing all winter long.
    After the pain has become an old known
friend, repeating itself, you can hold on to it.
    The power of fright, I think, is as much
as magnetic heat or gravity.
    After what is boundless: wind chimes,
fertile patches of the land,
the ochre symmetry of fields in fall,
the end of breath, the beginning
of shadow, the shadow of heat as it moves
the way the night heads west,
I take this road to arrive at its end
where the toll taker passes the night, reading.
    I feel the cupped heat
of his left hand as he inherits
change; on the road that is not his road
anymore I belong to whatever it is
which will happen to me.
    When I left this city I gave back
the metallic waking in the night, the signals
of barges moving coal up a slow river north,

After the Grand Perhaps

the movement of trains, each whistle
like a woodwind song of another age
passing, each ambulance would split a night
in two, lying in bed as a little girl,
a fear of being taken with the sirens
as they lit the neighborhood in neon, quick
as the fire as it takes fire
& our house goes up in night.
    After what is arbitrary: the hand grazing
something too sharp or fine, the word spoken
out of sleep, the buckling of the knees to cold,
the melting of the parts to want,
the design of the moon to cast
unfriendly light, the dazed shadow
of the self as it follows the self,
the toll taker's sorrow
that we couldn't have been more intimate.
    Which leads me back to the land,
the old wolves which used to roam on it,
the one light left on the small far hill
where someone must be living still.
    After life there must be life.

Notes

According to Herodotus, the ancient Egyptians believed that, after death, the human soul had to pass through various forms of incarnation for a period of 3,000 years. Plato, in *The Phaedrus,* set the period at 10,000 years (which the Philosophic Soul could reduce to a mere 3,000-year period). In *The Republic,* however, he calculates that the departed souls had to spend 1,000 years before returning to this world. In **Domestic Mysticism,** the formula of exile is derived from Empedocles, who reckoned the period of the soul's transmigration as "thrice ten-thousand seasons," or 2,500 years.

The child in **Birdie Africa,** Oyewolffe Momar Puim, was born in 1971 in Germantown. At the age of two, his mother took him from his father to join the MOVE cult in Philadelphia. All the disciples, headed by John Africa (Vincent Leaphart), changed their surnames to Africa; the child was called Birdie. In May of 1985 the police firebombed their tenement. Birdie was one of only two known to have survived the fire.

In **Real Life,** the "thirty-six things" refers to the French text, *The Thirty-Six Dramatic Situations,* written by Georges Polti in 1921, translated by Lucille Ray and published in 1977 by The Writer, Inc., Boston. According to Polti's theory, all tragic situations are based on 36 basic plots, and his analysis reduces the basis of all literature into such categories as "Fatal Imprudence" (17), "Daring Enterprise" (9), "Abduction" (16), "Obtaining" (12), "Obstacles to Love" (28), "Self-Sacrificing for an Ideal" (20).

The Future as a Cow is based on an interview with Manute Bol, the 7′7″ Sudanese basketball star who, in 1985, was the starting center for the University of Bridgeport basketball team. In "Sudan to Bridgeport: The Long Journey of Manute Bol," by David H. Van Biema *(People),* Bol said: "My father was a farmer. Not a big farmer. He made some money. He sold potatoes and tomatoes. He had about 150 cows. . . . When I want to get married to some girl, and her father says, 'I want 100 cows,' what are you going to do if you don't have the cows? That's why you keep cows. I took care of the cows. I looked for animals that would like to kill the cows. Lions, hyenas. Sometimes I talk out loud to keep them away. . . . Right now I play ball. I can stay here in this country and I don't have to sell my cows, because I like the cows like my father liked them. I'm going to school right now. I play now. I can't say the future is not a cow. The cow may be my future. I don't know."

Edward VI, the speaker in **Edward VI on the Seventh Day,** was the only son born to Henry VIII. He succeeded his father as King of England and Ireland at the age of nine. He died of consumption six years later in 1553.

In the early morning hours of Wednesday, October 14, 1987, Jessica Mc-Clure, of **Jessica, from the Well,** removed a flower pot which covered a hole in her aunt's backyard in Midland, Texas. The eighteen-month-old girl slipped down through an 8-inch-wide opening into an abandoned well shaft. She remained there until her rescue on Friday evening, fifty-eight hours later. Upon her emergence from the well, psychiatrists assured the American public through the media that Jessica, though physically battered from her ordeal, would have no psychological scarring, no memory of the event.

Hitchcock Blue is based on an article which describes a blue dinner party hosted by Alfred Hitchcock. Everything in the meal was tinted blue—blue steak, blue mashed potatoes, blue utensils, blue salad, blueberries. His guests were reported to have had no comment regarding the color of the meal; dining commenced as usual.

The girl in **Archaeology,** India Wood, at the age of thirteen, found a bone protruding from the ground near her home in Colorado Springs. Over a three-year period, she unearthed fragments of a well-preserved 150-million-year-old skeleton of a carnivorous *Allosaurus*. Piecemeal, she brought the bones home and reconstructed the dinosaur on her bedroom floor. The five-ton allosaur, thirty-five feet tooth to tail and fifteen feet tall, was placed on exhibition at the Denver Museum of Natural History.

In **The Beginning of the Beginning,** the line *I am afraid of what the world will do* is quoted from Thomas James' *Letter to a Stranger* (Houghton Mifflin, Boston, 1972).

The speaker in **Elective Mutes,** June Gibbons, is one of a set of identical twins born in 1963 at Steam Point, an RAF hospital in Aden. Beginning in their early childhood, she and her twin, Jennifer, refused to communicate with any adult; they became electively mute. As the sisters grew up together, they became more and more detached from the real world, eventually living and speaking in an invented world of poems, novels, and diaries based on the lives and rituals of their dolls. Eventually, their fantasies and languages became more symbiotic and more pathological. As they became impossibly and progressively intertwined and encoded, they began to turn on one another; they became arsonists, and eventually, they began to think of murdering one another. Now in their twenties, they are imprisoned in Broadmoor hospital for the criminally insane. All italics in the poem are quoted from the journals of June Gibbons, published in *The*

Notes

Silent Twins by Marjorie Wallace (Prentice Hall Press, Englewood Cliffs, New Jersey, 1986).

In **I Wish You Love,** the references to Josef pertain to the discovery and exhumation of a grave in Embu, Brazil, on June 6, 1985. An international team of forensic scientists in São Paulo announced that the skeleton, buried under the name of Wolfgang Gerhard, was actually that of the notorious Nazi fanatic, Dr. Josef Mengele. All italics in the poem are quoted from the Charles Trenet song "Que Reste-t-il de Nos Amours." The piece was published in 1946 and was later recorded in English by Marlene Dietrich under the title "I Wish You Love."

The title **Ten Years Apprenticeship in Fantasy** refers to John Keats' request to be given a decade in which to indulge himself, watching the world before writing it all down. The epigraph for the poem, taken from "Sleep and Poetry," is as follows: *O for ten years, that I may overwhelm / Myself in poesy; so I may do the deed / That my own soul has to itself decreed.*

The title **And So Long, I've Had You Fame** was taken from the last published interview with Marilyn Monroe. She said: "Fame will go by, and, so long, I've had you fame. If it goes by, I've always known it was fickle. So at least it's something I've experienced, but that's not where I live." The interview, written by Richard Meryman, appeared in *Life* in 1962. *Cursum Perficio* ("I am finishing my journey") was etched in a tile placed outside the front door of Monroe's home in Brentwood, California.

After the Grand Perhaps was inspired by these alleged final words of François Rabelais: "I am going to seek a grand perhaps; draw the curtain, the farce is played."

A Note About the Author

Lucie Brock-Broido is the author of two other collections of poetry, *The Master Letters* and *Trouble in Mind*. She is Director of Poetry in the School of the Arts at Columbia University. She has been the recipient of awards from the John Simon Guggenheim Foundation, the National Endowment for the Arts, and the American Academy of Arts and Letters. She lives in New York City and in Cambridge, Massachusetts.

A Note on the Type

This book was set in Granjon, a type named
in compliment to Robert Granjon but neither
a copy of a classic face nor an entirely
original creation. George W. Jones based his designs
on the type used by Claude Garamond (c. 1480–
1561) in his beautiful French books. Granjon more
closely resembles Garamond's own type than does
any of the various modern types that bear his name.

Robert Granjon began his career as type cutter in
1523. The boldest and most original designer of his
time, he was one of the first to practice the trade of
type founder apart from that of printer. Between
1557 and 1562 Granjon printed about twenty books
in types designed by himself, following, after the
fashion, the cursive handwriting of the time. These
types, usually known as *caractères de civilité,* he
himself called *lettres françaises,* as especially
appropriate to his own country.

Composed by Creative Graphics,
Allentown, Pennsylvania
Printed and bound by United Book Press,
Baltimore, Maryland
Designed by Harry Ford

Printed in the United States
by Baker & Taylor Publisher Services